Zen in the Art of Archery

Eugen Herrigel was a German professor who taught philosophy at the University of Tokyo between the Wars. He trained with a Zen Master for six years, and much of his experience during this period is contained in this book.

Zen in the Art of Archery

EUGEN HERRIGEL

Translated by R.F.C. Hull
Foreword by D.T. Suzuki

ARKANA

PENGUIN BOOKS

PENGUIN BOOKS

Published by the Penguin Group
Penguin Books Ltd, 80 Strand, London WC2R 0RL, England
Penguin Putnam Inc., 375 Hudson Street, New York, New York 10014, USA
Penguin Books Australia Ltd, 250 Camberwell Road, Camberwell, Victoria 3124, Australia
Penguin Books Canada Ltd, 10 Alcorn Avenue, Toronto, Ontario, Canada M4V 3B2
Penguin Books India (P) Ltd, 11 Community Centre, Panchsheel Park, New Delhi – 110 017, India
Penguin Books (NZ) Ltd, Cnr Rosedale and Airborne Roads, Albany, Auckland, New Zealand
Penguin Books (South Africa) (Pty) Ltd, 24 Sturdee Avenue, Rosebank 2196, South Africa

Penguin Books Ltd, Registered Offices: 80 Strand, London WC2R 0RL, England

www.penguin.com

This translation first published by Routledge & Kegan Paul 1953
Published in Arkana 1985

10

Translation copyright 1953 by Routledge & Kegan Paul
All rights reserved

Printed in England by Clays Ltd, St Ives plc

FOREWORD
By Daisetz Teitaro Suzuki

ONE OF the most significant features we notice in the practice of archery, and in fact of all the arts as they are studied in Japan and probably also in other Far Eastern countries, is that they are not intended for utilitarian purposes only or for purely aesthetic enjoyments, but are meant to train the mind; indeed, to bring it into contact with the ultimate reality. Archery is, therefore, not practised solely for hitting the target; the swordsman does not wield the sword just for the sake of outdoing his opponent; the dancer does not dance just to perform certain rhythmical movements of the body. The mind has first to be attuned to the Unconscious.

If one really wishes to be master of an art, technical knowledge of it is not enough. One has to transcend technique so that the art becomes an 'artless art' growing out of the Unconscious.

In the case of archery, the hitter and the hit are no longer two opposing objects, but are one reality. The archer ceases to be conscious of himself as the one who is engaged in hitting the bull's-eye which confronts him. This state of unconsciousness is realized only when, completely empty and rid of the self, he becomes one with the perfecting of his technical skill, though there is in it something of a quite different order which cannot be attained by any progressive study of the art.

What differentiates Zen most characteristically from all other teachings, religious, philosophical, or mystical, is that while it never goes out of our daily life, yet with all its practicalness and concreteness Zen has something in it which makes it stand aloof from the scene of worldly sordidness and restlessness.

Here we come to the connection between Zen and archery, and such other arts as swordsmanship, flower arrangement, the tea ceremony, dancing, and the fine arts.

Zen is the 'everyday mind', as was proclaimed by Baso (Ma-tsu, *died* 788); this 'everyday mind' is no more than 'sleeping when tired, eating when hungry'. As soon as wc reflect, deliberate, and conceptualise, the original unconsciousness is lost and a thought interferes. We no longer eat while eating, we no longer sleep while sleeping. The arrow is off the string but does not fly straight to the target, nor does the target stand where it is. Calculation which is miscalculation sets in. The whole business of archery goes the wrong way. The archer's confused mind betrays itself in every direction and every field of activity.

Man is a thinking reed but his great works are done when he is not calculating and thinking. 'Childlikeness' has to be restored after long years of training in the art of self-forgetfulness. When this is attained, man thinks yet he does not think. He thinks like the showers coming down from the sky; he thinks like the waves rolling on the ocean; he thinks like the stars illuminating the nightly heavens; he thinks like the green foliage shooting forth in the relaxing spring breeze. Indeed, he is the showers, the ocean, the stars, the foliage.

When a man reaches this stage of 'spiritual' development, he is a Zen artist of life. He does not need, like the painter, a canvas, brushes, and paints; nor does he require, like the archer, the bow and arrow and target, and other paraphernalia. He has his limbs, body, head, and other parts. His Zen-life expresses itself by means of all these 'tools' which are important to its manifestation. His hands and feet are the brushes and the whole universe is the canvas on which he depicts his life for seventy, eighty, or even ninety years. This picture is called 'history'.

Hoyen of Gosozen (died 1104) says: 'Here is a man who, turning the emptiness of space into a sheet of paper, the waves of the ocean into an inkwell, and Mount Sumeru into a brush, writes these five characters: so—shi—sai—rai—i.[1] To such, I spread my *zagu*[2] and make my profound bow.'

One may well ask, 'What does this fantastic pronouncement mean? Why is a person who can perform such a feat considered worthy of the utmost respect?' A Zen master would perhaps answer, 'I eat when hungry, I sleep when tired'. If he is nature-minded, he may say, 'It was fine yesterday and to-day it is raining'. For the reader,

[1] These five characters in Chinese, literally translated, mean 'the first patriarch's motive for coming from the west'. The theme is often taken up as a subject of *mondo*. It is the same as asking about the most essential thing in Zen. When this is understood, Zen is this body itself.

[2] *Zagu* is one of the articles carried by the Zen monk. It is spread before him when he bows to the Buddha or to the teacher.

Foreword

however, the question may still remain unsolved, 'Where is the archer?'

In this wonderful little book, Mr. Herrigel, a German philosopher who came to Japan and took up the practice of archery toward an understanding of Zen, gives an illuminating account of his own experience. Through his expression, the Western reader will find a more familiar manner of dealing with what very often must seem to be a strange and somewhat unapproachable Eastern experience.

DAISETZ T. ZUZUKI

Ipswich, Massachusetts
May 1953

PREFACE

In 1936 a lecture which I had delivered to the German-Japanese Society in Berlin appeared in the magazine *Nippon* under the title 'The Chivalrous Art of Archery'. I had given this lecture with the utmost reserve, for I had intended to show the close connection which exists between this art and Zen. And since this connection eludes precise description and real definition, I was fully conscious of the provisional nature of my attempt.

In spite of everything, my remarks aroused great interest. They were translated into Japanese in 1937, into Dutch in 1938, and in 1939 I received news—so far unconfirmed—that an Indian translation was being planned. In 1940 a much improved Japanese translation appeared together with an eyewitness account by Prof. Sozo Komachiya.

When Curt Weller, who published *The Great Liberation*, D. T. Suzuki's important book on Zen, and who is also bringing out a carefully planned series of Buddhist writings, asked me whether I agreed to a reprint of my lecture, I willingly gave my consent. But, in the conviction of having made further spiritual progress during the past ten years—and this means ten years of continual practice—and of being able to say rather better than before, with greater understanding and realization, what this 'mystical' art is about, I have resolved to set down my experiences in new form. Unforgettable memories and notes which I made at the time in connection with the archery lessons, stood me in good stead. And so I can well say that there is no word in this exposition which the Master would not have spoken, no image or comparison which he would not have used.

I have also tried to keep my language as simple as possible. Not only because Zen teaches and advocates the greatest economy of expression, but because I have found that what I cannot say quite simply and without recourse to mystic jargon has not become sufficiently clear and concrete even to myself.

To write a book on the essence of Zen itself is one of my plans for the near future.

EUGEN HERRIGEL

ZEN

IN THE ART OF ARCHERY

I

At first sight it must seem intolerably degrading for Zen—however the reader may understand this word—to be associated with anything so mundane as archery. Even if he were willing to make a big concession, and to find archer, distinguished as an 'art', he would scarcely feel inclined to look behind this art for anything more than a decidedly sporting form of prowess. He therefore expects to be told something about the amazing feats of Japanese trick-artists, who have the advantage of being able to rely on a time-honoured and unbroken tradition in the use of bow and arrow. For in the Far East it is only a few generations since the old means of combat were replaced by modern weapons, and familiarity in the handling of them by no means fell into disuse, but went on propagating itself, and has since been cultivated in ever widening circles. Might one not expect, therefore, a description of the special ways in which archery is pursued to-day as a national sport in Japan?

Nothing could be more mistaken than this expectation. By archery in the traditional sense, which he esteems as an art and honours as a national heritage, the Japanese does not understand a sport but, strange as this may sound at first, a religious ritual. And consequently, by the 'art' of archery he does not mean the ability of the sportsman, which can be controlled, more or less, by bodily exercises, but an ability whose origin is to be sought in spiritual exercises and whose aim consists in hitting a spiritual goal, so that fundamentally the marksman aims at himself and may even succeed in hitting himself.

This sounds puzzling, no doubt. What, the reader will say, are we to believe that archery, once practised for the contest of life and death, has not survived even as a sport, but has been degraded to a spiritual exercise? Of what use, then, are the bow and arrow and target? Does not this deny the manly old art and honest meaning of archery, and set up in its place something nebulous, if not positively fantastic?

It must, however, be borne in mind that the peculiar spirit of this art, far from having to be infused back into the use of bow and arrow in recent times, was always essentially bound up with them, and has emerged all the more forthrightly and convincingly now that it no longer has to prove itself in bloody contests. It is not true to say that the traditional technique of archery, since it is no longer of importance in fighting, has turned into a pleasant pastime and thereby been rendered innocuous. The 'Great Doctrine' of archery tells us something very different. According to it, archery is still a matter of life and death to the extent that it is a contest of the archer with himself; and this kind of contest is not a paltry substitute, but the foundation of all contests outwardly directed—for instance with a bodily opponent. In this contest of the archer with himself is revealed the secret essence of this art, and instruction in it does not suppress anything essential by waiving the utilitarian ends to which the practice of knightly contests was put.

Anyone who subscribes to this art to-day, therefore, will gain from its historical development the undeniable advantage of not being tempted to obscure his understanding of the 'Great Doctrine' by practical aims—even though he hides them from himself—and to make it perhaps altogether impossible. For access to the art—and the master archers of all times are agreed in this—is only granted to those who are 'pure' in heart, untroubled by subsidiary aims.

Should one ask, from this standpoint, how the Japanese Masters understand this contest of the archer with himself, and how they describe it, their answer would sound enigmatic in the extreme. For them the contest consists in the archer aiming at himself—and yet not at himself, in hitting himself—and yet not himself, and thus becoming simultaneously the aimer and the aim, the hitter and the hit. Or, to use some expressions which are nearest the heart of the Masters, it is necessary for the archer to become, in spite of himself, an unmoved centre. Then comes the supreme and ultimate miracle: art becomes 'artless', shooting becomes not-shooting, a shooting without bow and arrow; the teacher becomes a pupil again, the Master a beginner, the end a beginning, and the beginning perfection.

For Orientals these mysterious formulae are clear and familiar truths, but for us they are completely bewildering. We have therefore to go into this question more deeply. For some considerable time it has been no secret, even to us Europeans, that the Japanese arts go back for their inner form to a common root, namely Buddhism. This is as true of the art of archery as of ink painting, of the art of the theatre no less than the tea ceremony, the art of flower arrangement, and swordsmanship. All of them presuppose a spiritual attitude and each cultivates it in its own way—an attitude which, in its most exalted form, is characteristic of Buddhism and determines the nature of the priestly type of man. I do not mean Buddhism in the ordinary sense, nor am I concerned here with the decidedly speculative form of Buddhism, which, because of its allegedly accessible literature, is the only one we know in Europe and even claim to understand. I mean Dhyana Buddhism, which is known in Japan as 'Zen' and is not speculation at all but immediate experience of what, as the bottomless ground of Being, cannot be apprehended by intellectual means, and cannot be conceived or interpreted even after the most unequivocal and incontestable experiences: one knows it by not knowing it. For the sake of those crucial experiences Zen Buddhism has struck out on paths which, through methodical immersion in oneself, lead to one's becoming aware, in the deepest ground of the soul, of the unnamable Groundlessness and Qualitylessness —nay more, to one's becoming one with it. And this, with respect to archery and expressed in very tentative and on that account possibly misleading language, means that the spiritual exercises, thanks to which alone the technique of archery becomes an art and, if all goes well, perfects itself as the 'artless art', are mystical exercises, and accordingly archery can in no circumstances mean accomplishing anything outwardly with bow and arrow, but only inwardly, with oneself. Bow and arrow are only a pretext for something that could just as well happen without them, only the way to a goal, not the goal itself, only helps for the last decisive leap.

In view of all this, nothing would be more desirable than that one should be able to lay hands on expositions by Zen Buddhists as an aid to understanding. These are in fact not lacking. In his *Essays In Zen Buddhism*,[1] D. T. Suzuki has succeeded in showing that Japanese culture and Zen are inti-

[1] *Essays in Zen Buddhism*, First Series, 1927; Second Series, 1950; Third Series, 1953.

mately connected and that Japanese art, the spiritual attitude of the Samurai, the Japanese way of life, the moral, aesthetic and to a certain extent even the intellectual life of the Japanese owe their peculiarities to this background of Zen and cannot be properly understood by anybody not acquainted with it.

The exceedingly important work of Suzuki and the researches of other Japanese scholars have aroused widespread interest. It is generally admitted that Dhyana Buddhism, which was born in India and, after undergoing profound changes, reached full development in China, to be finally adopted by Japan, where it is cultivated as a living tradition to this day, has disclosed unsuspected ways of existence which it is of the utmost importance for us to understand.

Despite all the efforts of Zen experts, however, the insight afforded to us Europeans into the essence of Zen has remained exceedingly scanty. As though it resisted deeper penetration, after a few steps one's groping *intuition* comes up against insurmountable barriers. Wrapped in impenetrable darkness, Zen must seem the strangest riddle which the spiritual life of the East has ever devised: insoluble and yet irresistibly attractive.

The reason for this painful feeling of inaccessibility lies, to some extent, in the style of exposition that has hitherto been adopted for Zen. No reasonable person would expect a Zen adept to do more than hint at the experiences which have liberated and changed him, or to attempt to describe the unimaginable and ineffable 'Truth' by which he now lives. In this respect Zen is akin to pure introspective mysticism. Unless we enter into mystic experiences by direct participation, we remain outside, turn and twist as we may. This law, which all genuine mysticism obeys, allows of no exceptions. It is no contradiction that there exists a plethora of Zen texts regarded as sacred. They have the peculiarity of disclosing their life-giving meaning only to those who have shown themselves worthy of the crucial experiences and who can therefore extract from these texts confirmation of what they themselves already possess and are independently of them. To the inexperienced, on the other hand, they remain not only dumb—how could he ever be in a position to read between the lines?—but will infallibly lead him into the most hopeless spiritual confusion, even if he approaches them with wariness and selfless devotion. Like all mysticism, Zen can only be understood by one who is himself a mystic and is therefore not tempted to gain by underhand methods what the mystical experience withholds from him.

Yet the man who is transformed by Zen, and who has passed through the 'fire of truth', leads far too convincing a life for it to be overlooked. So it is not asking too much if, driven by a feeling of spiritual affinity, and desirous of finding a way to the nameless power which can work such miracles—for the merely curious have no right to demand anything—we expect the Zen adept at least to describe the way that leads to the goal. No mystic and no student of Zen is, at first step, the man he can become through self-perfection. How much has still to be conquered and left behind before he finally lights upon the truth! How often is he tormented on the way by the desolate feeling that he is attempting the impossible! And yet this impossible will one day have become possible and even self-evident. Is there not room for the hope, then, that a careful description of this long and difficult road will allow us at least one thing: to ask whether we wish to travel it?

Such descriptions of the way and its stations are almost entirely lacking in Zen literature. This is partly due to the fact that the Zen adept has an insuperable objection to giving any kind of instructions for the happy life. He knows from personal experience that nobody can stay the course without conscientious guidance from a skilled teacher and without the help of a Master. No less decisive, on the other hand, is the fact that his experiences, his conquests and spiritual transformations, so long as they still remain 'his', must be conquered and transformed again and again until everything 'his' is annihilated. Only in this way can he attain a basis for experiences which, as the 'all-embracing Truth' rouse him to a life that is no longer his everyday, personal life. He lives, but what lives is no longer himself.

From this standpoint we can understand why the Zen adept shuns all talk of himself and his progress. Not because he thinks it immodest to talk, but because he regards it as a betrayal of Zen. Even to make up his mind to say anything about Zen itself costs him grave heart-searchings. He has before him the warning example of one of the greatest Masters, who, on being asked what Zen was, maintained an unmoving silence, as though he had not heard the question. How then could any adept feel tempted to render an account of what he has thrown away and no longer misses?

In these circumstances, I should be shirking my responsibilities if I confined myself to a string of paradoxes and took refuge behind a barrage of high-sounding words. For it was my intention to throw light on the nature of Zen as it affects one of the arts on which it has set its stamp. This light is certainly not illumination in the sense fundamental to Zen, but at least shows that there must be something behind the impenetrable walls of mist, and which, like summer lightning, heralds the distant storm. So understood, the art of archery is rather like a preparatory school for Zen, for it enables the beginner to gain a clearer view, through the works of his own hands, of events which are not in themselves intelligible. Objectively speaking, it would be entirely possible to make one's way to Zen from any one of the arts I have named.

However, I think I can achieve my aim most effectively by describing the course which a pupil of the art of archery has to complete. To be more precise, I shall try to summarize the six-year course of instruction I received from one of the greatest Masters of this art during my stay in Japan. So it is my own experiences which authorize me in this undertaking. In order to make myself intelligible at all—for even this preparatory school holds riddles enough—I have no alternative but to recollect in detail all the resistances I had to overcome, all the inhibitions I had to fight down, before I succeeded in penetrating into the spirit of the Great Doctrine. I speak about myself only because I see no other way of reaching the goal I have set before me. For the same reason I shall confine my account to essentials, so as to make them stand out more clearly. I consciously refrain from describing the setting in which the instruction took place, from conjuring up scenes that have fixed themselves in my memory, and above all from sketching a picture of the Master—however tempting all this may be. Everything must hinge on the art of archery, which, I sometimes feel, is even more difficult to expound than to learn; and the exposition must be carried to the point where we begin to discern those far-off horizons behind which Zen lives and breathes.

II

WHY I took up Zen, and for this purpose set out to learn the art of archery, needs some explanation. Even as a student I had, as though driven by a secret urge, been preoccupied with mysticism, despite the mood of the times, which had little use for such interests. For all my exertions, however, I became increasingly aware that I could only approach these esoteric writings from the outside; and though I knew how to circle around what one may call the primordial mystic phenomenon, I was unable to leap over the line which surrounded the mystery like a high wall. Nor could I find exactly what I sought in the extensive literature of mysticism, and, disappointed and discouraged, I gradually came to realize that only the truly detached can understand what is meant by 'detachment', and that only the contemplative, who is completely empty and rid of the self, is ready to 'become one' with the 'transcendent Deity'. I had realized, therefore, that there is and can be no other way to mysticism than the way of personal experience and suffering, and that, if this premise is lacking, all talk about it is so much empty chatter. But—how does one become a mystic? How attain the state of real, and not just imaginary, detachment? Is there still a way to it even for those who are separated by the abyss of the centuries from the great Masters? For the modern man, who has grown up under totally different conditions? Nowhere did I find anything approaching satisfactory answers to my questions, even though I was told about the stages and stations of a way that promised to lead to the goal. To tread this way, I lacked the precise methodical instructions which might substitute for a Master, at least for part of the journey. But would such instructions, even if there were any, suffice? Is it not more probable that, at best, they only create a readiness to receive something which even the best method cannot provide, and that the mystical experience therefore cannot be induced by any disposition known to man? However I looked at it, I found myself confronted by locked doors, and yet I could not refrain from constantly rattling at the handles. But the longing persisted, and, when it grew weary, the longing for this longing.

When, therefore, I was asked—I had in the meantime become a lecturer at a university—whether I would like to teach philosophy at the University of Tokyo, I welcomed this opportunity of getting to know the country and people of Japan with especial joy, if only because it held out the prospect of my making contact with Buddhism and hence with an introspective practice of mysticism. For this much I had already heard, that there was in Japan a carefully guarded and living tradition of Zen, an art of instruction that had been tested over the centuries, and, most important of all, teachers of Zen astonishingly well versed in the art of spiritual guidance.

Scarcely had I begun to find my way about in the new milieu when I set out to realize my desire. I at once met with embarrassed refusals. Never yet, I was told, had any European seriously concerned himself with Zen, and since Zen repudiated the least trace of 'teaching', it was not to be expected that it would satisfy me 'theoretically'. It cost me many wasted hours before I succeeded in making them understand why I wished to devote myself specifically to the non-speculative form of Zen. Thereupon I was informed that it was quite hopeless for a European to attempt to penetrate into this realm of spiritual life—perhaps the strangest which the Far East has to offer—unless he began by learning one of the Japanese arts associated with Zen.

The thought of having to go through a kind of preparatory schooling did not deter me. I felt ready to go to any length if only there were some hope of my getting a bit nearer to Zen; and a roundabout way, however wearisome, seemed better to me than no way at all. But to which of the arts named for this purpose should I subscribe? My wife, after a little hesitation, decided for flower arrangement and painting, while the art of archery seemed more suitable for me, on the—as it later turned out—completely erroneous assumption that my experiences in rifle and pistol shooting would be to my advantage.

I begged one of my colleagues, Sozo Komachiya, a professor of jurisprudence who had been taking lessons in archery for twenty years and who was rightly regarded as the best exponent of this art at the university, to enter my name as a pupil with his former teacher, the celebrated Master Kenzo

Awa. The Master at first refused my request, saying that he had once been misguided enough to instruct a foreigner and had regretted the experience ever since. He was not prepared to make concessions a second time, in order to spare the pupil the burden of the peculiar spirit of this art. Only when I protested that a Master who took his job so seriously could well treat me as his youngest pupil, seeing that I wished to learn this art not for pleasure but for the sake of the 'Great Doctrine', did he accept me as his pupil, together with my wife, since it has long been customary in Japan for girls to be instructed in this art, and since the Master's wife and two daughters were diligent practitioners.

And so began the long and strenuous course of instruction, in which our friend Mr. Komachiya, who pleaded our cause so obstinately and almost stood guarantor for us, participated as interpreter. At the same time my good fortune in being invited to attend my wife's lessons in flower arrangement and painting held out the prospect of my winning a still broader basis of understanding through constant comparison of these mutually complementary arts.

III

THAT THE way of the 'artless art' is not easy to follow we were to learn during the very first lesson. The Master began by showing us various Japanese bows, explaining that their extraordinary elasticity was due to their peculiar construction and also to the material from which they are generally made, namely bamboo. But it seemed even more important to him that we should note the noble form which the bow—it is over six feet long—assumes as soon as it is strung, and which appears the more surprising the further the bow is drawn. When drawn to its full extent, the bow encloses the 'All' in itself, explained the Master, and that is why it is important to learn how to draw it properly. Then he grasped the best and strongest of his bows and, standing in a ceremonious and dignified attitude, let the lightly drawn bowstring fly back several times. This produces a sharp crack mingled with a deep thrumming, which one never afterwards forgets when one has heard it only a few times: so strange is it, so thrillingly does it grip the heart. From ancient times it has been credited with the secret power of banishing evil spirits, and I can well believe that this interpretation has struck root in the whole Japanese people. After this significant introductory act of purification and consecration the Master commanded us to watch him closely. He placed, or 'nocked', an arrow on the string, drew the bow so far that I was afraid it would not stand up to the strain of embracing the All, and loosed the arrow. All this looked not only very beautiful, but quite effortless. He then gave us his instructions: 'Now you do the same, but remember that archery is not meant to strengthen the muscles. When drawing the string you should not exert the full strength of your body, but must learn to let only your two hands do the work, while your arm and shoulder muscles remain relaxed, as though they looked on impassively. Only when you can do this will you have fulfilled one of the conditions that make the drawing and the shooting "spiritual".' With these words he gripped my hands and slowly guided

31

them through the phases of the movement which they would have to execute in the future, as if accustoming me to the feel of it.

Even at the first attempt with a medium-strong practice-bow I noticed that I had to use considerable force to bend it. This is because the Japanese bow, unlike the European sporting bow, is not held at shoulder level, in which position you can, as it were, press yourself into it. Rather, as soon as the arrow is nocked, the bow is held up with arms at nearly full stretch, so that the archer's hands are somewhere above his head. Consequently, the only thing he can do is to pull them evenly apart to left and right, and the further apart they get the more they curve downwards, until the left hand, which holds the bow, comes to rest at eye level with the arm outstretched, while the right hand, which draws the string, is held with arm bent above the right shoulder, so that the tip of the three-foot arrow sticks out a little beyond the outer edge of the bow—so great is the span. In this attitude the archer has to remain for a while before loosing the shot. The strength needed for this unusual method of holding and drawing the bow caused my hands to start trembling after a few moments, and my breathing became more and more laboured. Nor did this get any better during the weeks that followed. The drawing continued to be a difficult business, and despite the most diligent practice refused to become 'spiritual'. To comfort myself, I hit upon the thought that there must be a trick somewhere which the Master for some reason would not divulge, and I staked my ambition on its discovery.

Grimly set on my purpose, I continued practising. The Master followed my efforts attentively, quietly corrected my strained attitude, praised my enthusiasm, reproved me for wasting my strength, but otherwise let me be. Only, he always touched on a sore spot when, as I was drawing the bow, he called out to me to 'Relax! Relax!'—a word he had learned in the meantime—though he never lost his patience and politeness. But the day came when it was I who lost patience and brought myself to admit that I absolutely could not draw the bow in the manner prescribed.

'You cannot do it', explained the Master, 'because you do not breathe right. Press your breath down gently after breathing in, so that the abdominal wall is tightly stretched, and hold it there for a while. Then breathe out as slowly and evenly as possible, and, after a short pause, draw a quick breath of air again—out and in continually, in a rhythm that will gradually settle itself. If it is done properly, you will feel the shooting becoming easier every day. For through this breathing you will not only discover the source of all spiritual strength but will also cause this source to flow more abundantly, and to pour more easily through your limbs the more relaxed you are.' And as if to prove it, he drew his strong bow and invited me to step behind him and feel his arm muscles. They were indeed quite relaxed, as though they were doing no work at all.

The new way of breathing was practised, without bow and arrow at first, until it came naturally. The slight feeling of discomfort noticeable in the beginning was quickly overcome. The Master attached so much importance to breathing out as slowly and steadily as possible to the very end, that, for better practice and control, he made us combine it with a humming note. Only when the note had died away with the last expiring breath were we allowed to draw air again. The breathing in, the Master once said, binds and combines, by holding your breath you make everything go right, and the breathing out loosens and completes by overcoming all limitations. But we could not understand that yet.

The Master now went on to relate the breathing, which had not of course been practised for its own sake, to archery. The unified process of drawing and shooting was divided into sections: grasping the bow, nocking the arrow, raising the bow, drawing and remaining at the point of highest tension, loosing the shot. Each of them began with breathing in, was sustained by firm holding of the down-pressed breath, and ended with breathing out. The result was that the breathing fell into place spontaneously and not only accentuated the individual positions and hand-movements, but wove them together in a rhythmical sequence depending, for each of us, on the state of his breathing-capacity. In spite of its being divided into parts the entire process seemed like a living thing wholly contained in itself, and not even remotely comparable to a gymnastic exercise, to which bits can be added or taken away without its meaning and character being thereby destroyed.

I cannot think back to those days without recalling, over and over again, how difficult I found it, in the beginning, to get my breathing to work out right. Though I breathed in technically the right way, whenever I tried to keep my arm and shoulder muscles relaxed while drawing the bow the muscles of my legs stiffened all the more violently, as though my life depended on a firm foothold and secure stance, and as though, like Antaeus, I had to draw strength from the ground. Often the Master had no alternative but to pounce quick as lightning on one of my leg muscles and press it in a particularly sensitive spot. When, to excuse myself, I once remarked that I was conscientiously making an effort to keep relaxed, he replied: 'That's just the trouble, you make an effort to think about it. Concentrate entirely on your breathing, as if you had nothing else to do!' It took me a considerable time before I succeeded in doing what the Master wanted. But—I succeeded. I learned to lose myself so effortlessly in the breathing that I sometimes had the feeling that I myself was not breathing but—strange as this may sound —being breathed. And even when, in hours of thoughtful reflection, I struggled against this bold idea, I could no longer doubt that the breathing held out all that the Master had promised. Now and then, and in the course of time more and more frequently, I managed to draw the bow and keep it drawn until the moment of release while remaining completely relaxed in body, without my being able to say how it happened. The qualitative difference between these few successful shots and the innumerable failures was so convincing that I was ready to admit that now at last I understood what was meant by drawing the bow 'spiritually'.

So that was it: not a technical trick I had tried in vain to pick up, but liberating breath-control with new and far-reaching possibilities. I say this not without misgiving, for I well know how great is the temptation to succumb to a powerful influence and, ensnared in self-delusion, to overrate the importance of an experience merely because it is so unusual. But despite all equivocation and sober reserve, the results obtained by the new breathing —for in time I was able to draw even the strong bow of the Master with muscles relaxed—were far too definite to be denied.

In talking it over with Mr. Komachiya, I once asked him why the Master had looked on so long at my futile efforts to draw the bow 'spiritually', why he had not insisted on the correct breathing right from the the start. 'A great Master', he replied, 'must also be a great teacher. With us the two things go hand in hand. Had he begun the lessons with breathing exercises, he would never have been able to convince you that you owe them anything decisive. You had to suffer shipwreck through your own efforts before you were ready to seize the lifebelt he threw you. Believe me, I know from my own experience that the Master knows you and each of his pupils much better than we know ourselves. He reads in the souls of his pupils more than they care to admit.'

IV

To be able to draw the bow 'spiritually' after a year, that is, with a kind of effortless strength, is no very startling achievement. And yet I was well content, for I had begun to understand why the system of self-defence whereby one brings one's opponent to the ground unexpectedly giving way, with effortless resilience, to his passionately delivered attack, thus turning his own strength against him, is known as 'the gentle art'. Since the remotest times its symbol has been the yielding and yet unconquerable water, so that Lao-tzu could say with profound truth that right living is like water, which 'of all things the most yielding can overwhelm that which is of all things most hard'.[1] Moreover, the saying of the Master

[1] *The Way and its Power*, tr. by Arthur Waley, London, 1934, p. 197.

went round in school, that 'whoever makes good progress in the beginning has all the more difficulties later on'. For me the beginning had been far from easy: was I not entitled, therefore, to feel confident in the face of what was to come, and the difficulties of which I was already beginning to suspect?

The next thing to be learned was the 'loosing' of the arrow. Up to now we had been allowed to do this haphazard: it stood in parenthesis, as it were on the margin of the exercises. And what happened to the arrow was even more a matter of indifference. So long as it pierced the roll of pressed straw which served the double purpose of target and sandbank, honour was deemed to have been satisfied. To hit it was no great feat, since we were only ten paces away from it at most.

Hitherto I had simply let go of the bowstring when the hold at the point of highest tension had become unendurable, when I felt I had to give way if my parted hands were not forcibly to be pulled together again. The tension is not in any sense painful. A leather glove with a stiffened and thickly padded thumb guards against the pressure of the string becoming uncomfortable and prematurely shortening the hold at the point of highest tension.

When drawing, the thumb is wrapped round the bowstring immediately below the arrow, and tucked in. The first three fingers are gripped over it firmly, and at the same time give the arrow a secure hold. Loosing therefore means opening the fingers that grip the thumb and setting it free. Through the tremendous pull of the string the thumb is wrenched from its position, stretched out, the string whirrs and the arrow flies. When I had loosed hitherto, the shot had never gone off without a powerful jerk, which made itself felt in a visible shaking of my whole body and affected the bow and arrow as well. That there could be no possibility of a smooth and, above all, certain shot goes without saying; it was bound to 'wobble'.

'All that you have learned hitherto', said the Master one day when he found nothing more to object to in my relaxed manner of drawing the bow, 'was only a preparation for loosing the shot. We are now faced with a new and particularly difficult task, which brings us to a new stage in the art of archery.' So saying, the Master gripped his bow, drew it and shot. Only now, when expressly watching out for it, did I observe that though the right hand of the Master, suddenly opened and released by the tension, flew back with a jerk, it did not cause the least shaking of the body. The right arm, which before the shot had formed an acute angle, was jerked open but ran gently back into full extension. The unavoidable jerk had been cushioned and neutralized.

If the force of the discharge did not betray itself in the sharp 'thup' of the quivering bowstring and in the penetrative power of the arrow, one would never suspect its existence. At least in the case of the Master the loose looked so simple and undemanding that it might have been child's play.

The effortlessness of a performance for which great strength is needed is a spectacle of whose aesthetic beauty the East has an exceedingly sensitive and grateful appreciation. But ever more important to me—and at that stage I could hardly think otherwise—was the fact that the certainty of hitting seemed to depend on the shot's being smoothly loosed. I knew from rifle-shooting what a difference it makes to jerk away, if only slightly, from the line of sight. All that I had learned and achieved so far only became intelligible to me from this point of view: relaxed drawing of the bow, relaxed holding at the point of highest tension, relaxed loosing of the shot, relaxed cushioning of the recoil—did not all this serve the grand purpose of hitting the target, and was not this the reason why we were learning archery with so much trouble and patience? Why then had the Master spoken as if the process we were now concerned with far exceeded everything we had practised and accustomed ourselves to up till now?

However that may be, I went on practising diligently and conscientiously according to the Master's instructions, and yet all my efforts were in vain. Often it seemed to me that I had shot better before, when I loosed the shot at random without thinking about it. Above all I noticed that I could not open the right hand, and particularly the fingers gripping the thumb, without exertion. The result was a jerk at the moment of release, so that the arrow wobbled. Still less was I capable of cushioning the suddenly freed hand. The Master continued undeterred to demonstrate the correct loose; undeterred I sought to do like him—with the sole result that I grew more uncertain than ever. I seemed like the centipede which was unable to stir from the spot after trying to puzzle out in what order its feet ought to go.

The Master was evidently less horrified by my failure than I myself. Did he know from experience that it would come to this? 'Don't think of what you have to do, don't consider how to carry it out!' he exclaimed. 'The shot will only go smoothly when it takes the archer himself by surprise. It must be as if the bowstring suddenly cut through the thumb that held it. You mustn't open the right hand on purpose.'

There followed weeks and months of fruitless practice. I could take my standard again and again from the way the Master shot, see with my own eyes the nature of the correct loose; but not a single one succeeded. If, waiting in vain for the shot, I gave way to the tension because it began to be unendurable, then my hands were slowly pulled together, and the shot came to nothing. If I grimly resisted the tension till I was gasping for breath, I could only do so by calling on the arm and shoulder muscles for aid. I then stood there immobilized —like a statue, mocked the Master—but tense, and my relaxedness was gone.

Perhaps it was chance, perhaps it was deliberately arranged by the Master, that we one day found ourselves together over a cup of tea. I seized on this opportunity for a discussion and poured my heart out.

'I understand well enough', I said, 'that the hand mustn't be opened with a jerk if the shot is not to be spoiled. But however I set about it, it always goes wrong. If I clench my hand as tightly as possible, I can't stop it shaking when I open my fingers. If, on the other hand, I try to keep it relaxed, the bowstring is torn from my grasp before the full stretch is reached—unexpectedly, it is true, but still too early. I am caught between these two kinds of failure and see no way of escape.' 'You must hold the drawn bowstring', answered the Master, 'like a little child holding the proffered finger. It grips it so firmly that one marvels at the strength of the tiny fist. And when it lets the finger go, there is not the slightest jerk. Do you know why? Because a child doesn't think: I will now let go of the finger in order to grasp this other thing. Completely un-selfconsciously, without purpose, it turns from one to the other, and we would say that it was playing with the things, were it not equally true that the things are playing with the child.'

'Maybe I understand what you are hinting at with this comparison,' I remarked. 'But am I not in an entirely different situation? When I have drawn the bow, the moment comes when I feel: unless the shot comes at once I shan't be able to endure the tension. And what happens then?

Merely that I get out of breath. So I must loose the shot whether I want to or not, because I can't wait for it any longer.'

'You have described only too well', replied the Master, 'where the difficulty lies. Do you know why you cannot wait for the shot and why you get out of breath before it has come? The right shot at the right moment does not come because you do not let go of yourself. You do not wait for fulfilment, but brace yourself for failure. So long as that is so, you have no choice but to call forth something yourself that ought to happen independently of you, and so long as you call it forth your hand will not open in the right way—like the hand of a child: it does not burst open like the skin of a ripe fruit.'

I had to admit to the Master that this interpretation made me more confused than ever. 'For ultimately', I said, 'I draw the bow and loose the shot in order to hit the target. The drawing is thus a means to an end, and I cannot lose sight of this connection. The child knows nothing of this, but for me the two things cannot be disconnected.'

'The right art', cried the Master, 'is purposeless, aimless! The more obstinately you try to learn how to shoot the arrow for the sake of hitting the goal, the less you will succeed in the one and the further the other will recede. What stands in your way is that you have a much too wilful will. You think that what you do not do yourself does not happen.'

'But you yourself have told me often enough that archery is not a pastime, not a purposeless game, but a matter of life and death!'

'I stand by that. We master archers say: one shot —one life! What this means, you cannot yet understand. But perhaps another image will help you, which expresses the same experience. We master archers say: with the upper end of the bow the archer pierces the sky, on the lower end, as though attached by a thread, hangs the earth. If the shot is loosed with a jerk there is a danger of the thread snapping. For purposeful and violent people the rift becomes final, and they are left in the awful centre between heaven and earth.'

'What must I do, then?' I asked thoughtfully.

'You must learn to wait properly.'

'And how does one learn that?'

'By letting go of yourself, leaving yourself and everything yours behind you so decisively that nothing more is left of you but a purposeless tension.'

'So I must become purposeless—on purpose?' I heard myself say.

'No pupil has ever asked me that, so I don't know the right answer.'

'And when do we begin these new exercises?'

'Wait until it is time.'

V

THIS CONVERSATION—the first intimate talk I had had since the beginning of my instruction—puzzled me exceedingly. Now at last we had touched on the theme for whose sake I had undertaken to learn archery. Was not this letting go of oneself, of which the Master had spoken, a stage on the way to emptiness and detachment? Had I not reached the point where the influence of Zen on the art of archery began to make itself felt? What the relation might be between the purpose-less waiting-capacity and the loosing of the shot at the right moment, when the tension spontaneously fulfilled itself, I could not at present fathom. But why try to anticipate in thought what only experience can teach? Was it not high time to drop this unfruitful habit? How often I had silently envied all those pupils of the Master who, like children, let him take them by the hand and lead them. How delightful it must be to be able to do this without reserve. Such an attitude need not necessarily lead to indifference and spiritual stagnation. Might not children at least ask questions?

During the next lesson the Master—to my disappointment—went on with the previous exercises: drawing, holding, and loosing. But all this encouragement availed nothing. Although I tried, in accordance with his instructions, not to give way to the tension, but to struggle beyond it as though no limits were set by the nature of the bow; although I strove to wait until the tension simultaneously fulfilled and loosed itself in the shot—despite all my efforts every shot miscarried; bewitched, botched, wobbling. Only when it became clear that it was not only pointless to continue these exercises but positively dangerous, since I was oppressed more and more by a premonition of failure, did the Master break off and begin on a completely new tack.

'When you come to the lessons in the future', he warned us, 'you must collect yourselves on your way here. Focus your minds on what happens in the practice-hall. Walk past everything without noticing it, as if there were only one thing in the

world that is important and real, and that is
archery!'

The process of letting go of oneself was likewise divided into separate sections which had to
be worked through carefully. And here too the
Master contented himself with brief hints. For the
performance of these exercises it is sufficient that
the pupil should understand, or in some cases
merely guess, what is demanded of him. Hence
there is no need to conceptualize the distinctions
which are traditionally expressed in images. And
who knows whether these images, born of centuries of practice, may not go deeper than all our
carefully calculated knowledge?

The first step along this road had already been
taken. It had led to a loosening of the body, without which the bow cannot be properly drawn. If
the shot is to be loosed right, the physical loosening
must now be continual in a mental and spiritual
loosening, so as to make the mind not only agile,
but free: agile because of its freedom, and free because of its original agility; and this original agility
is essentially different from everything that is
usually understood by mental agility. Thus, between these two states of bodily relaxedness on the
one hand and spiritual freedom on the other there

is a difference of level which cannot be overcome by breath-control alone, but only by withdrawing from all attachments whatsoever, by becoming utterly egoless: so that the soul, sunk within itself, stands in the plenitude of its nameless origin.

The demand that the door of the senses be closed is not met by turning energetically away from the sensible world, but rather by a readiness to yield without resistance. In order that this actionless activity may be accomplished instinctively, the soul needs an inner hold, and it wins it by concentrating on breathing. This is performed consciously and with a conscientiousness that borders on the pedantic. The breathing in, like the breathing out, is practised again and again by itself with the utmost care. One does not have to wait long for results. The more one concentrates on breathing, the more the external stimuli fade into the background. They sink away in a kind of muffled roar which one hears with only half an ear at first, and in the end one finds it no more disturbing than the distant roar of the sea, which, once one has grown accustomed to it, is no longer perceived. In due course one even grows immune to larger stimuli, and at the same time detachment from them becomes easier and quicker. Care has only to be taken that the body is relaxed whether standing, sitting, or lying, and if one then concentrates on breathing one soon feels oneself shut in by impermeable layers of silence. One only knows and feels that one breathes. And, to detach oneself from this feeling and knowing, no fresh decision is required, for the breathing slows down of its own accord, becomes more and more economical in the use of breath, and finally, slipping by degrees into a blurred monotone, escapes one's attention altogether.

This exquisite state of unconcerned immersion in oneself is not, unfortunately, of long duration. It is liable to be disturbed from inside. As though sprung from nowhere, moods, feelings, desires, worries and even thoughts incontinently rise up, in a meaningless jumble, and the more far-fetched and preposterous they are, and the less they have to do with that on which one has fixed one's consciousness, the more tenaciously they hang on. It is as though they wanted to avenge themselves on consciousness for having, through concentration, touched upon realms it would otherwise never reach. The only successful way of rendering this disturbance inoperative is to keep on breathing quietly and unconcernedly, to enter into friendly relations with whatever appears on the scene, to accustom oneself to it, to look at it equably and at last grow weary of looking. In this way one gradually gets into a state which resembles the melting drowsiness on the verge of sleep.

To slip into it finally is the danger that has to be avoided. It is met by a peculiar leap of concentration, comparable perhaps to the jolt which a man who has stayed up all night gives himself when he knows that his life depends on all his senses being alert; and if this leap has been successful but a single time it can be repeated with certainty. With its help the soul is brought to the point where it vibrates of itself in itself—a serene pulsation which can be heightened into the feeling, otherwise experienced only in rare dreams, of extraordinary lightness, and the rapturous certainty of being able to summon up energies in any direction, to intensify or to release tensions graded to a nicety.

This state, in which nothing definite is thought, planned, striven for, desired or expected, which aims in no particular direction and yet knows itself capable alike of the possible and the impossible, so unswerving is its power—this state, which is at bottom purposeless and egoless, was called by the Master truly 'spiritual'. It is in fact charged with spiritual awareness and is therefore also called 'right presence of mind'. This means that the mind or spirit is present everywhere, because it is nowhere attached to any particular place. And it can remain present because, even when related to this or that object, it does not cling to it by reflection and thus lose its original mobility. Like water filling a pond, which is always ready to flow off again, it can work its inexhaustible power because it is free, and be open to everything because it is empty. This state is essentially a primordial state, and its symbol, the empty circle, is not empty of meaning for him who stands within it.

Out of the fulness of this presence of mind, disturbed by no ulterior motive, the artist who is released from all attachment must practise his art. But if he is to fit himself self-effacingly into the creative process, the practice of the art must have the way smoothed for it. For if, in his self-immersion, he saw himself faced with a situation into which he could not leap instinctively, he would first have to bring it to consciousness. He would then enter again into all the relationships from which he had detached himself; he would be like one wakened, who considers his programme for the day, but not like an Awakened One who lives and works in the primordial state. It would never appear to him as if the individual parts of the creative process were being played into his hands by a higher power; he would never experience how intoxicatingly the vibrancy of an event is communicated to him who is himself only a vibration, and how everything that he does is done before he knows it.

The necessary detachment and self-liberation, the inward-turning and intensification of life until full presence of mind is reached, are therefore not left to chance or to favourable conditions, the less so as the more depends on them, and least of all are they abandoned to the process of creation itself—which already demands all the artist's powers—in the hope that the desired concentration will appear of its own accord. Before all doing and creating, before ever he begins to devote and adjust himself to his task, the artist summons forth this presence of mind and makes sure of it through practice. But, from the time he succeeds in capturing it not merely at rare intervals but in having it at his finger tips in a few moments, the concentration, like the breathing, is brought into connection with archery. In order to slip the more easily into the process of drawing the bow and loosing the shot, the archer, kneeling to one side and beginning to concentrate, rises to his feet, ceremoniously steps up to the target and, with a deep obeisance, offers the bow and arrow like consecrated gifts, then nocks the arrow, raises the bow, draws it and waits in an attitude of supreme spiritual alertness. After the lightning release of the arrow and the tension, the archer remains in the posture adopted immediately following the shot until, after slowly expelling his breath, he is forced to draw air again. Then only does he let his arms sink, bows to the target and, if he has no more shots to discharge, steps quietly into the background.

Archery thus becomes a ceremony which exemplifies the 'Great Doctrine'.

Even if the pupil does not, at this stage, grasp the true significance of his shots, he at least understands why archery cannot be a sport, a gymnastic exercise. He understands why the technically learnable part of it must be practised to the point of repletion. If everything depends on the archer's becoming purposeless and effacing himself in the event, then its outward realization must occur automatically, in no further need of the controlling or reflecting intelligence.

VI

I T IS this mastery of form that the Japanese
method of instruction seeks to inculcate. Practice, repetition, and repetition of the repeated
with ever increasing intensity are its distinctive
features for long stretches of the way. At least this
is true of all the traditional arts. Demonstration,
example; intuition, imitation—that is the fundamental relationship of instructor to pupil, although
with the introduction of new educational subjects
during the last few decades European methods of
instruction have also gained a foothold and been
applied with undeniable understanding. How is it
that in spite of the initial enthusiasm for everything
new, the Japanese arts have remained in essence
untouched by these educational reforms?

It is not easy to give an answer to this question.
Yet the attempt must be made, even if only

sketchily, with a view to throwing more light on the style of instruction and the meaning of imitation.

The Japanese pupil brings with him three things: good education, passionate love for his chosen art, and uncritical veneration of his teacher. The teacher-pupil relationship has belonged since ancient times to the basic commitments of life and therefore presupposes, on the part of the teacher, a high responsibility which goes far beyond the scope of his professional duties.

Nothing more is required of the pupil, at first, than that he should conscientiously copy what the teacher shows him. Shunning long-winded instructions and explanations, the latter contents himself with perfunctory commands and does not reckon on any questions from the pupil. Impassively he looks on at the blundering efforts, not even hoping for independence or initiative, and waits patiently for growth and ripeness. Both have time: the teacher does not harass, and the pupil does not overtax himself.

Far from wishing to waken the artist in the pupil prematurely, the teacher considers it his first task to make him a skilled artisan with sovereign control of his craft. The pupil follows out this intention with untiring industry. As though he had no higher aspirations he bows under his burden with a kind of obtuse devotion, only to discover in the course of years that forms which he perfectly masters no longer oppress but liberate. He grows daily more capable of following any inspiration without technical effort, and also of letting inspiration come to him through meticulous observation. The hand that guides the brush has already caught and executed what floated before the mind at the same moment as the mind began to form it, and in the end the pupil no longer knows which of the two—mind or hand—was responsible for the work.

But, to get that far, for the skill to become 'spiritual', a concentration of all the physical and psychic forces is needed, as in the art of archery—which, as will be seen from the following examples, cannot under any circumstances be dispensed with.

A painter seats himself before his pupils. He examines his brush and slowly makes it ready for use, carefully rubs ink, straightens the long strip of paper that lies before him on the mat, and finally, after lapsing for a while into profound concentration, in which he sits like one inviolable, he produces with rapid, absolutely sure strokes a picture which, capable of no further correction and needing none, serves the class as a model.

A flower master begins the lesson by cautiously untying the bast which holds together the flowers and sprays of blossom, and laying it to one side carefully rolled up. Then he inspects the sprays one by one, picks out the best after repeated examination, cautiously bends them into the form which exactly corresponds with the role they are to play, and finally places them together in an exquisite vase. The completed picture looks just as if the Master had guessed what Nature had glimpsed in dark dreams.

In both these cases—and I must confine myself to them—the Masters behave as if they were alone. They hardly condescend to give their pupils a glance, still less a word. They carry out the preliminary movements musingly and composedly, they efface themselves in the process of shaping and creating, and to both the pupils and themselves it seems like a self-contained event from the first opening manœuvres to the completed work. And indeed the whole thing has such expressive power that it affects the beholder like a picture.

But why doesn't the teacher allow these preliminaries, unavoidable though they are, to be done by an experienced pupil? Does it lend wings to his visionary and plastic powers if he rubs the ink himself, if he unties the bast so elaborately instead of cutting it and carelessly throwing it away? And what impels him to repeat this process at every single lesson, and, with the same remorseless insistence, to make his pupils copy it without the least alteration? He sticks to this traditional custom because he knows from experience that the preparations for working put him simultaneously in the right frame of mind for creating. The meditative repose in which he performs them gives him that vital loosening and equability of all his powers, that collectedness and presence of mind, without which no right work can be done. Sunk without purpose in what he is doing, he is brought face to face with that moment when the work, hovering before him in ideal lines, realizes itself as if of its own accord. As with the steps and postures in archery, so here in modified form other preparations have the same meaning. And only where this does not apply, as for instance with religious dancers and actors, are the self-recollection and self-immersion practised *before* they appear on the stage.

As in the case of archery, there can be no question but that these arts are ceremonies. More clearly than the teacher could express it in words, they tell the pupil that the right frame of mind for the artist is only reached when the preparing and the creating, the technical and the artistic, the material and the spiritual, the project and the object, flow together without a break. And here he finds a new theme for emulation. He is now required to exercise perfect control over the various ways of concentration and self-effacement. Imitation, no longer applied to objective contents which anybody can copy with a little good will, becomes looser, nimbler, more spiritual. The pupil sees himself on the brink of new possibilities, but discovers at the same time that their realization does not depend in the slightest degree on his good will.

Assuming that his talent can survive the increasing strain, there is one scarcely avoidable danger that lies ahead of the pupil on his road to mastery. Not the danger of wasting himself in idle self-gratification—for the East has no aptitude for this cult of the ego—but rather the danger of getting stuck in his achievement, which is confirmed by his success and magnified by his renown: in other words, of behaving as if the artistic existence were a form of life that bore witness to its own validity.

The teacher foresees this danger. Carefully and with the adroitness of a psychopomp he seeks to head the pupil off in time and to detach him from himself. This he does by pointing out, casually and as though it were scarcely worth a mention in view of all that the pupil has already learned, that all right doing is accomplished only in a state of true selflessness, in which the doer cannot be present any longer as 'himself'. Only the spirit is present, a kind of awareness which shows no trace of ego-hood and for that reason ranges without limit through all the distances and depths, with 'eyes that hear and with ears that see'.

Thus the teacher lets his pupil voyage onward through himself. But the pupil, with growing receptiveness, lets the teacher bring to view something of which he has often heard but whose reality is only now beginning to become tangible on the basis of his own experiences. It is immaterial what name the teacher gives it, whether indeed he names it at all. The pupil understands him even when he keeps silent.

The important thing is that an inward movement is thereby initiated. The teacher pursues it, and, without influencing its course with further instructions which would merely disturb it, helps the pupil in the most secret and intimate way he knows by direct transference of the spirit, as it is called in Buddhist circles. 'Just as one uses a burning candle to light others with', so the teacher transfers the spirit of the right art from heart to heart, that it may be illumined. If such should be granted to the pupil, he remembers that more important than all outward works, however attractive, is the inward work which he has to accomplish if he is to fulfil his vocation as an artist.

The inward work, however, consists in his turning the man he is, and the self he feels himself and perpetually finds himself to be, into the raw material of a training and shaping whose end is mastery. In it, the artist and the human being meet in something higher. For mastery proves its validity as a form of life only when it dwells in the boundless Truth and, sustained by it, becomes the art of the origin. The Master no longer seeks, but finds. As an artist he is the hieratic man; as a man, the artist, into whose heart, in all his doing and not-doing, working and waiting, being and not-being, the Buddha gazes. The man, the art, the work—it is all one. The art of the inner work, which unlike the outer does not forsake the artist, which he does not 'do' and can only 'be', springs from depths of which the day knows nothing.

Steep is the way to mastery. Often nothing keeps the pupil on the move but his faith in his teacher, whose mastery is now beginning to dawn on him. He is a living example of the inner work, and he convinces by his mere presence.

How far the pupil will go is not the concern of the teacher and Master. Hardly has he shown him the right way when he must let him go on alone. There is only one thing more he can do to help him endure his loneliness: he turns him away from himself, from the Master, by exhorting him to go further than he himself has done, and to 'climb on the shoulders of his teacher'.

Wherever his way may take him, the pupil, though he may lose sight of his teacher, can never forget him. With a gratitude as great as the uncritical veneration of the beginner, as strong as the saving faith of the artist, he now takes his Master's place, ready for any sacrifice. Countless examples down to the recent past testify that this gratitude far exceeds the measure of what is customary among mankind.

VII

DAY BY day I found myself slipping more easily into the ceremony which sets forth the 'Great Doctrine' of archery, carrying it out effortlessly or, to be more precise, feeling myself being carried through it as in a dream. Thus far the Master's predictions were confirmed. Yet I could not prevent my concentration from flagging at the very moment when the shot ought to come. Waiting at the point of highest tension not only became so tiring that the tension relaxed, but so agonizing that I was constantly wrenched out of my self-immersion and had to direct my attention to discharging the shot. 'Stop thinking about the shot!' the Master called out. 'That way it is bound to fail.' 'I can't help it,' I answered, 'the tension gets too painful.'

'You only feel it because you haven't really let

go of yourself. It is all so simple. You can learn from an ordinary bamboo leaf what ought to happen. It bends lower and lower under the weight of snow. Suddenly the snow slips to the ground without the leaf having stirred. Stay like that at the point of highest tension until the shot falls from you. So, indeed, it is: when the tension is fulfilled, the shot *must* fall, it must fall from the archer like snow from a bamboo leaf, before he even thinks it.'

In spite of everything I could do or did not do, I was unable to wait until the shot 'fell'. As before, I had no alternative but to loose it on purpose. And this obstinate failure depressed me all the more since I had already passed my third year of instruction. I will not deny that I spent many gloomy hours wondering whether I could justify this waste of time, which seemed to bear no conceivable relationship to anything I had learned and experienced so far. The sarcastic remark of a countryman of mine, that there were important pickings to be made in Japan besides this beggarly art, came back to me, and though I had dismissed it at the time, his query as to what I intended to do with my art if ever I learned it no longer seemed to me so entirely absurd.

The Master must have felt what was going on in my mind. He had, so Mr. Komachiya told me later, tried to work through a Japanese introduction to philosophy in order to find out how he could help me from a side I already knew. But in the end he had laid the book down with a cross face, remarking that he could now understand that a person who interested himself in such things would naturally find the art of archery uncommonly difficult to learn.

We spent our summer holidays by the sea, in the solitude of a quiet, dreamy landscape distinguished for its delicate beauty. We had taken our bows with us as the most important part of our equipment. Day out and day in I concentrated on loosing the shot. This had become an *idée fixé*, which caused me to forget more and more the Master's warning that we should not practise anything except self-detaching immersion. Turning all the possibilities over in my mind, I came to the conclusion that the fault could not lie where the Master suspected it: in lack of purposelessness and egolessness, but in the fact that the fingers of the right hand gripped the thumb too tight. The longer I had to wait for the shot, the more convulsively I pressed them together without thinking. It was at this point, I told myself, that I must set to work. And ere long I had found a simple and obvious solution to this problem. If, after drawing the bow, I cautiously eased the pressure of the fingers on the thumb, the moment came when the thumb, no longer held fast, was torn out of position as if spontaneously: in this way a lightning loose could be made and the shot would obviously 'fall like snow from a bamboo leaf'. This discovery recommended itself to me not least on account of its beguiling affinity with the technique of rifle-shooting. There the index finger is slowly crooked until an ever diminishing pressure overcomes the last resistance.

I was able to convince myself very quickly that I must be on the right track. Almost every shot went off smoothly and unexpectedly, to my way of thinking. Naturally I did not overlook the reverse side of this triumph: the precision work of the right hand demanded my full attention. But I comforted myself with the hope that this technical solution would gradually become so habitual that it would require no further notice from me, and that the day would come when, thanks to it, I should be in a position to loose the shot, self-obliviously and unconsciously, at the moment of highest tension, and that in this case the technical ability would spiritualize itself. Waxing more and more confident in this conviction I silenced the protest that rose up in me, ignored the contrary counsels from my wife, and went away with the satisfying feeling of having taken a decisive step forward.

The very first shot I let off after the recommencement of the lessons was, to my mind, a brilliant success. The loose was smooth, unexpected. The Master looked at me for a while and then said hesitantly, like one who can scarcely believe his eyes: 'Once again, please!' My second shot seemed to me even better than the first. The Master stepped up to me without a word, took the bow from my hand, and sat down on a cushion, his back towards me. I knew what that meant, and withdrew.

The next day Mr. Komachiya informed me that the Master declined to instruct me any further because I had tried to cheat him. Horrified beyond measure by this interpretation of my behaviour, I explained to Mr. Komachiya why, in order to avoid marking time forever, I had hit upon this method of loosing the shot. On his interceding for me, the Master was finally prepared to give in, but made the continuation of the lessons conditional upon my express promise never to offend again against the spirit of the 'Great Doctrine'.

If profound shame had not cured me, the Master's behaviour would certainly have done so. He did not mention the incident by so much as a word, but only said quite quietly: 'You see what comes of not being able to wait without purpose in the state of highest tension. You cannot even learn to do this without continually asking yourself: Shall I be able to manage it? Wait patiently, and see what comes—and how it comes!'

I pointed out to the Master that I was already in my fourth year and that my stay in Japan was limited.

'The way to the goal is not to be measured! Of what importance are weeks, months, years?'

'But what if I have to break off half way?' I asked.

'Once you have grown truly egoless you can break off at any time. Keep on practising that.'

And so we began again from the very beginning, as if everything I had learned hitherto had become useless. But the waiting at the point of highest tension was no more successful than before, as if it were impossible for me to get out of the rut.

One day I asked the Master: 'How can the shot be loosed if "I" do not do it?'

' "It" shoots,' he replied.

'I have heard you say that several times before, so let me put it another way: How can I wait self-obliviously for the shot if "I" am no longer there?'

' "It" waits at the highest tension.'

'And who or what is this "It"?'

'Once you have understood that, you will have no further need of me. And if I tried to give you a clue at the cost of your own experience, I should be the worst of teachers and should deserve to be sacked! So let's stop talking about it and go on practising.'

Weeks went by without my advancing a step. At the same time I discovered that this did not disturb me in the least. Had I grown tired of the whole business? Whether I learned the art or not, whether I experienced what the Master meant by 'It' or not, whether I found the way to Zen or not —all this suddenly seemed to have become so remote, so indifferent, that it no longer troubled me. Several times I made up my mind to confide in the Master, but when I stood before him I lost courage; I was convinced that I should never hear anything but the monotonous answer: 'Don't ask, practise!' So I stopped asking, and would have liked to stop practising, too, had not the Master held me inexorably in his grip. I lived from one day to the next, did my professional work as best I might, and in the end ceased to bemoan the fact that all my efforts of the last few years had become meaningless.

Then, one day, after a shot, the Master made a deep bow and broke off the lesson, 'Just then "It" shot!' he cried, as I stared at him bewildered. And when I at last understood what he meant I couldn't suppress a sudden whoop of delight.

'What I have said', the Master told me severely, 'was not praise, only a statement that ought not to touch you. Nor was my bow meant for you, for you are entirely innocent of this shot. You remained this time absolutely self-oblivious and without purpose in the highest tension, so that the shot fell from you like a ripe fruit. Now go on practising as if nothing had happened.'

Only after a considerable time did more right shots occasionally come off, which the Master signalized by a deep bow. How it happened that they loosed themselves without my doing anything, how it came about that my tightly closed right hand suddenly flew back wide open, I could not explain then and I cannot explain to-day. The fact remains that it did happen, and that alone is important. But at least I got to the point of being able to distinguish, on my own, the right shots from the failures. The qualitative difference is so great that it cannot be overlooked once it has been experienced. Outwardly, for the observer, the right shot is distinguished by the cushioning of the right hand as it is jerked back, so that no tremor runs through the body. Again, after wrong shots the pent-up breath is expelled explosively, and the next breath cannot be drawn quickly enough. After right shots the breath glides effortlessly to its end, whereupon air is unhurriedly breathed in again. The heart continues to beat evenly and quietly, and with concentration undisturbed one can go straight on to the next shot. But inwardly, for the archer himself, right shots have the effect of making him feel that the day has just begun. He feels in the mood for all right doing, and, what is perhaps even more important, for all right not-doing. Delectable indeed is this state. But he who has it, said the Master with a subtle smile, would do well to have it as though he did not have it. Only unbroken equanimity can accept it in such a way that it is not afraid to come back.

VIII

'WELL, AT least we've got over the worst,' I said to the Master, when he announced one day that we were going on to some new exercises. 'He who has a hundred miles to walk should reckon ninety as half the journey,' he replied, quoting the proverb. 'Our new exercise is shooting at a target.'

What had served till now as a target and arrow-catcher was a roll of straw on a wooden stand, which one faced at a distance of two arrows laid end to end. The target, on the other hand, set up at a distance of about sixty feet, stands on a high and broadly based bank of sand which is piled up against three walls, and, like the hall in which the archer stands, is covered by a beautifully curved tile roof. The two halls are connected by high wooden partitions which shut off from the outside the space where such strange things happen.

The Master proceeded to give us a demonstration of target-shooting: both arrows were embedded in the black of the target. Then he bade us perform the ceremony exactly as before, and, without letting ourselves be put off by the target, wait at the highest tension until the shot 'fell'. The slender bamboo arrows flew off in the right direction, but failed to hit even the sandbank, still less the target, and buried themselves in the ground just in front of it.

'Your arrows do not carry,' observed the Master, 'because they do not reach far enough spiritually. You must act as if the goal were infinitely far off. For master archers it is a fact of common experience that a good archer can shoot further with a medium-strong bow than an unspiritual archer can with the strongest. It does not depend on the bow, but on the presence of mind, on the vitality and awareness with which you shoot. In order to unleash the full force of this spiritual awareness, you must perform the ceremony differently: rather as a good dancer dances. If you do this, your movements will spring from the centre, from the seat of right breathing. Instead of reeling off the ceremony like something learned by heart, it will then be as if you were creating it under the inspiration of the moment, so that dance and dancer are one and the same. By performing the ceremony like a religious dance, your spiritual awareness will develop its full force.'

I do not know how far I succeeded in 'dancing' the ceremony and thereby activating it from the centre. I no longer shot too short, but I still failed to hit the target. This prompted me to ask the Master why he had never yet explained to us how to take aim. There must, I supposed, be a relation of sorts between the target and the tip of the arrow, and hence an approved method of sighting which makes hitting possible.

'Of course there is,' answered the Master, 'and you can easily find the required aim yourself. But if you hit the target with nearly every shot you are nothing more than a trick archer who likes to show off. For the professional who counts his hits, the target is only a miserable piece of paper which he shoots to bits. The 'Great Doctrine' holds this to be sheer devilry. It knows nothing of a target which is set up at a definite distance from the archer. It only knows of the goal, which cannot be aimed at technically, and it names this goal, if it names it at all, the Buddha.' After these words, which he spoke as though they were self-evident, the Master told us to watch his eyes closely as he shot. As when performing the ceremony, they were almost closed, and we did not have the impression that he was sighting.

Obediently we practised letting off our shots without taking aim. At first I remained completely unmoved by where my arrows went. Even occasional hits did not excite me, for I knew that so far as I was concerned they were only flukes. But in the end this shooting into the blue was too much for me. I fell back into the temptation to worry. The Master pretended not to notice my disquiet, until one day I confessed to him that I was at the end of my tether.

'You worry yourself unnecessarily,' the Master comforted me. 'Put the thought of hitting right out of your mind! You can be a Master even if every shot does not hit. The hits on the target are only the outward proof and confirmation of your purposelessness at its highest, of your egolessness, your self-abandonment, or whatever you like to call this state. There are different grades of mastery, and only when you have made the last grade will you be sure of not missing the goal.'

'That is just what I cannot get into my head,' I answered. 'I think I understand what you mean by the real, inner goal which ought to be hit. But how it happens that the outer goal, the disc of paper, is hit without the archer's taking aim, and that the hits are only outward confirmations of inner events—that correspondence is beyond me.'

'You are under an illusion', said the Master after a while, 'if you imagine that even a rough understanding of these dark connections would help you. These are processes which are beyond the reach of understanding. Do not forget that even in Nature there are correspondences which cannot be understood, and yet are so real that we have grown accustomed to them, just as if they could not be any different. I will give you an example which I have often puzzled over. The spider dances her web without knowing that there are flies who will get caught in it. The fly, dancing nonchalantly on a sunbeam, gets caught in the net without knowing what lies in store. But through both of them "It" dances, and inside and outside are united in this dance. So, too, the archer hits the target without having aimed—more I cannot say.'

Much as this comparison occupied my thoughts —though I could not of course think it to a satisfactory conclusion—something in me refused to be mollified and would not let me go on practising unworried. An objection, which in the course of weeks had taken on more definite outline, formulated itself in my mind. I therefore asked: 'Is it not at least conceivable that after all your years of practice you involuntarily raise the bow and arrow with the certainty of a sleepwalker, so that, although you do not consciously take aim when drawing it, you must hit the target—simply cannot fail to hit it?'

The Master, long accustomed to my tiresome questions, shook his head. 'I do not deny', he said after a short silence, 'that there may be something in what you say. I do stand facing the goal in such a way that I am bound to see it, even if I do not intentionally turn my gaze in that direction. On the other hand I know that this seeing is not enough, decides nothing, explains nothing, for I see the goal as though I did not see it.'

'Then you ought to be able to hit it blindfolded,' I jerked out.

The Master turned on me a glance which made me fear that I had insulted him and then said: 'Come to see me this evening.'

I seated myself opposite him on a cushion. He handed me tea, but did not speak a word. So we sat for a long while. There was no sound but the singing of the kettle on the hot coals. At last the Master rose and made me a sign to follow him. The practice hall was brightly lit. The Master told me to put a taper, long and thin as a knitting needle in the sand in front of the target, but not to switch on the light in the target sand. It was so dark that I could not even see its outlines, and if the tiny flame of the taper had not been there, I might perhaps have guessed the position of the target, though I could not have made it out with any precision. The Master 'danced' the ceremony. His first arrow shot out of dazzling brightness into deep night. I knew from the sound that it had hit the target. The second arrow was a hit, too. When I switched on the light in the target-stand, I discovered to my amazement that the first arrow was lodged full in the middle of the black, while the second arrow had splintered the butt of the first and ploughed through the shaft before embedding itself beside it. I did not dare to pull the arrows out separately, but carried them back together with the target. The Master surveyed them critically. 'The first shot', he then said, 'was no great feat, you will think, because after all these years I am so familiar with my target-stand that I must know even in pitch darkness where the target is. That may be, and I won't try to pretend otherwise. But the second arrow which hit the first—what do you make of that? I at any rate know that it is not "I" who must be given credit for this shot. "It" shot and "It" made the hit. Let us bow to the goal as before the Buddha!'

The Master had evidently hit me, too, with both arrows: as though transformed over night, I no longer succumbed to the temptation of worrying about my arrows and what happened to them. The Master strengthened me in this attitude still further by never looking at the target, but simply keeping his eye on the archer, as though that gave him the most suitable indication of how the shot had fallen out. On being questioned, he freely admitted that this was so, and I was able to prove for myself again and again that his sureness of judgment in this matter was no whit inferior to the sureness of his arrows. Thus, through deepest concentration, he transferred the spirit of his art to his pupils, and I am not afraid to confirm from my own experience, which I doubted long enough, that the talk of immediate communication is not just a figure of speech but a tangible reality. There was another form of help which the Master communicated to us at that time, and which he likewise spoke of as immediate transference of the spirit. If I had been continually shooting badly, the Master gave a few shots with my bow. The improvement was startling: it was as if the bow let itself be drawn differently, more willingly, more understandingly. This did not happen only with me. Even his oldest and most experienced pupils, men from all walks of life, took this as an established fact and were astonished that I should ask questions like one who wished to make quite sure. Similarly, no master of swordsmanship can be moved from his conviction that each of the swords fashioned with so much hard work and infinite care takes on the spirit of the swordsmith, who therefore sets about his work in ritual costume. Their experiences are far too striking, and they themselves far too skilled for them not to perceive how a sword reacts in their hands.

One day the Master cried out the moment my shot was loosed: 'It is there! Bow down to the goal!' Later, when I glanced towards the target—unfortunately I couldn't help myself—I saw that the arrow had only grazed the edge. 'That was a right shot,' said the Master decisively, 'and so it must begin. But enough for to-day, otherwise you will take special pains with the next shot and spoil the good beginning.' Occasionally several of these right shots came off in close succession and hit the target, besides of course the many more that failed. But if ever the least flicker of satisfaction showed in my face the Master turned on me with unwonted fierceness. 'What are you thinking of?' he would cry. 'You know already that you should not grieve over bad shots; learn now not to rejoice over the good ones. You must free yourself from the buffetings of pleasure and pain, and learn to rise above them in easy equanimity, to rejoice as though not you but another had shot well. This, too, you must practise unceasingly—you cannot conceive how important it is.'

During these weeks and months I passed through the hardest schooling of my life, and though the discipline was not always easy for me to accept, I gradually came to see how much I was indebted to it. It destroyed the last traces of any preoccupation with myself and the fluctuations of my mood. 'Do you now understand', the Master asked me one day after a particularly good shot, 'what I mean by "It shoots", "It hits"?'

'I'm afraid I don't understand anything more at all,' I answered, 'even the simplest things have got in a muddle. Is it "I" who draws the bow, or is it the bow that draws me into the state of highest tension? Do "I" hit the goal, or does the goal hit me? Is "It" spiritual when seen by the eyes of the body, and corporeal when seen by the eyes of the spirit—or both or neither? Bow, arrow, goal and and ego, all melt into one another, so that I can no longer separate them. And even the need to separate has gone. For as soon as I take the bow and shoot, everything becomes so clear and straightforward and so ridiculously simple. . . .'

'Now at last', the Master broke in, 'the bowstring has cut right through you.'

IX

MORE THAN five years went by, and then the Master proposed that we pass a test. 'It is not just a question of demonstrating your skill,' he explained. 'An even higher value is set on the spiritual deportment of the archer, down to his minutest gesture. I expect you above all not to let yourself be confused by the presence of spectators, but to go through the ceremony quite unperturbed, as though we were by ourselves.'

Nor, during the weeks that followed, did we work with the test in mind; not a word was said about it, and often the lesson was broken off after a few shots. Instead, we were given the task of performing the ceremony at home, executing its steps and postures with particular regard to right breathing and deep concentration.

We practised in the manner prescribed and discovered that hardly had we accustomed ourselves to dancing the ceremony without bow and arrow when we began to feel uncommonly concentrated after the first steps. This feeling increased the more care we took to facilitate the process of concentration by relaxing our bodies. And when, at lesson time, we again practised with bow and arrow, these home exercises proved so fruitful that we were able to slip effortlessly into the state of 'presence of mind'. We felt so secure in ourselves that we looked forward to the day of the test and the presence of spectators with equanimity.

We passed the test so successfully that the Master had no need to crave indulgence of the spectators with an embarrassed smile, and were awarded diplomas on the spot, each inscribed with the degree of mastery in which we stood. The Master brought the proceedings to an end by giving two masterly shots in robes of surpassing magnificence. A few days later my wife, in an open contest, was awarded the master title in the art of flower arrangement.

From then on the lessons assumed a new face. Contenting himself with a few practice shots, the Master went on to expound the 'Great Doctrine' in relation to the art of archery, and to adapt it to the stage we had reached. Although he dealt in mysterious images and dark comparisons, the meagrest hints were sufficient for us to understand what it was about. He dwelt longest on the 'artless art' which must be the goal of archery if it is to reach perfection. 'He who can shoot with the horn of the hare and the hair of the tortoise, and can hit the centre without bow (horn) and arrow (hair), he alone is Master in the highest sense of the word —Master of the artless art. Indeed, he is the artless art itself and thus Master and No-Master in one. At this point archery, considered as the unmoved movement, the undanced dance, passes over into Zen.'

When I asked the Master how we could get on without him on our return to Europe, he said: 'Your question is already answered by the fact that I made you take a test. You have now reached a stage where teacher and pupil are no longer two persons, but one. You can separate from me any time you wish. Even if broad seas lie between us, I shall always be with you when you practise what you have learned. I need not ask you to keep up your regular practising, not to discontinue it on any pretext whatsoever, and to let no day go by without your performing the ceremony, even without bow and arrow, or at least without having breathed properly. I need not ask you because I know that you can never give up this spiritual archery. Do not ever write to me about it, but send me photographs from time to time so that I can see how you draw the bow. Then I shall know everything I need to know.

'I must only warn you of one thing. You have become a different person in the course of these years. For this is what the art of archery means: a profound and far-reaching contest of the archer with himself. Perhaps you have hardly noticed it yet, but you will feel it very strongly when you meet your friends and acquaintances again in your own country: things will no longer harmonize as before. You will see with other eyes and measure with other measures. It has happened to me too, and it happens to all who are touched by the spirit of this art.'

In farewell, and yet not in farewell, the Master handed me his best bow. 'When you shoot with this bow you will feel the spirit of the Master near you. Give it not into the hands of the curious! And when you have passed beyond it, do not lay it up in remembrance! Destroy it, so that nothing remains but a heap of ashes.'

X

AFTER ALL this, I fear the suspicion will have grown up in the minds of many readers that, since archery is no longer of any importance in man-to-man contests, it has survived merely as a highly sophisticated form of spirituality and has thus become sublimated in a not very healthy way. And I can hardly blame them for thinking so.

It must therefore be emphasized once again that the Japanese arts, including the art of archery, have not come under the influence of Zen only in recent times, but have been under its influence for centuries. Indeed, a master archer of those far-off days, if put to the test, would not have been able to make any statements about the nature of his art radically different from those made by a master to-day, for whom the 'Great Doctrine' is a living reality. Throughout the centuries the spirit of this art has remained the same—as little alterable as Zen itself.

In order to dispel any lingering doubts—which as I know from my own experience, are understandable enough—I propose, for the sake of comparison, to cast a glance at another of these arts, whose martial significance even under present conditions cannot be denied: the art of swordsmanship. I make this attempt not only because Master Awa was a fine 'spiritual' swordsman as well, and occasionally pointed out to me the striking resemblance between the experiences of master archers and master swordsmen, but, even more, because there exists a literary document of the highest importance dating from feudal times, when chivalry was in full flower and master swordsmen had to demonstrate their prowess in the most irrevocable way, at the risk of their lives. This is a treatise by the great Zen master Takuan, entitled 'The Unmoved Understanding', where the connection of Zen with the art of swordsmanship and with the practice of the sword contest is dealt with at considerable length. I do not know whether it is the only document to expound the 'Great Doctrine' of swordsmanship in such detail and with so much originality; still less do I know whether there are similar testimonies with regard to the art of archery. However that may be, it is a great stroke of luck that Takuan's report has been preserved, and a great service on D. T. Suzuki's part to have translated this letter to a famous swordmaster more or less unabridged, and thus made it available to a wide circle of readers.[1] Arranging and summarizing the material in my own way, I shall try to explain as clearly and succinctly as possible what one understood by swordsmanship in the past, and what in the unanimous opinion of the great masters one has to understand by it to-day.

---

[1] Suzuki, Daisetz Teitaro, *Zen Buddhism and its Influence on Japanese Culture*. Kyoto: The Eastern Buddhist Society, 1938.

XI

AMONG SWORDMASTERS, on the basis of their own and their pupils' experience, it is taken as proved that the beginner, however strong and pugnacious he is, and however courageous and fearless he may be at the outset, loses not only his lack of self-consciousness, but his self-confidence, as soon as he starts taking lessons. He gets to know all the technical possibilities by which his life may be endangered in combat, and although he soon becomes capable of straining his attention to the utmost, of keeping a sharp watch on his opponent, of parrying his thrusts correctly and making effective lunges, he is really worse off than before, when, half in jest and half in earnest, he struck about him at random under the inspiration of the moment and as the joy of battle suggested. He is now forced to admit that he is at the mercy of everyone who is stronger, more nimble and more practised than he. He sees no other way open to him except ceaseless practise, and his instructor too has no other advice to give him for the present. So the beginner stakes everything on surpassing the others and even himself. He acquires a brilliant technique, which gives him back some of his lost self-confidence, and thinks he is drawing nearer and nearer to the desired goal. The instructor, however thinks differently—and rightly so, avers Takuan, since all the skill of the beginner only leads to his 'heart being snatched away by the sword'.

Yet the initial instruction cannot be imparted in any other way; it is thoroughly suited to the beginner. All the same it does not lead to the goal, as the instructor knows only too well. That the pupil does not become a swordmaster, despite his zeal and even despite his inborn skill, is understandable enough. But why is it that he, who has long since learned not to let himself be swept away by the heat of battle, but to keep a cool head, to conserve his strength, and who now feels inured to long-drawn combats and can hardly find an opponent to match him in all his circle—why is it that, judged by the highest standards, he fails at the last moment and makes no headway?

The reason, according to Takuan, is that the pupil cannot stop watching his opponent and his swordplay; that he is always thinking how he can best come at him, waiting for the moment when he is off his guard. In short, he relies all the time on his art and knowledge. By so doing, Takuan says, he loses his 'presence of heart': the decisive thrust always comes too late and he is unable to 'turn his opponent's sword against him'. The more he tries to make the brilliance of his swordplay dependent on his own reflection, on the conscious utilization of his skill, on his fighting experience and tactics, the more he inhibits the free 'working of the heart'. What is to be done? How does skill become 'spiritual', and how does sovereign control of technique turn into master swordplay? Only, so we are informed, by the pupil becoming purposeless and egoless. He must be taught to be detached not only from his opponent but from himself. He must pass through the stage he is still at and leave it behind him for good, even at the risk of irretrievable failure. Does not this sound as nonsensical as the demand that the archer should hit without taking aim, that he should completely lose sight of the goal and his intention to hit it? It is worth remembering, however, that the master swordsmanship whose essence Takuan describes has vindicated itself in a thousand contests.

The instructor's business is not to show the way itself, but to enable the pupil to get the feel of this way to the goal by adapting it to his individual peculiarities. He will therefore begin by training him to avoid thrusts instinctively, even when they take him completely by surprise. D. T. Suzuki describes in a delicious anecdote, the exceedingly original method employed by one instructor to submit himself to this far from easy task:

'The Japanese fencing master sometimes uses the Zen method of training. Once, when a disciple came to a master to be disciplined in the art of fencing, the master, who was in retirement in his mountain hut, agreed to undertake the task. The pupil was made to help him gather wood for kindling, draw water from the nearby spring, split wood, make the fire, cook rice, sweep the rooms and the garden, and generally look after his household affairs. There was no regular or technical teaching in the art. After some time the young man became dissatisfied, for he had not come to work as a servant to the old gentleman, but to learn the art of swordsmanship. So one day he approached the master and asked him to teach him.

The master agreed. The result was that the young man could not do any piece of work with any feeling of safety. For when he began to cook rice early in the morning, the master would appear and strike him from behind with a stick. When he was in the midst of his sweeping, he would be feeling the same blow from somewhere, from an unknown direction. He had no peace of mind, he had to be always on the *qui vive*. Some years passed before he could successfully dodge the blow from whatever source it might come. But the master was not quite satisfied with him yet. One day the master was found cooking his own vegetables over an open fire. The pupil took it into his head to avail himself of this opportunity. Taking up his big stick, he let it fall on the head of the master, who was then stooping over the cooking pan to stir its contents. But the pupil's stick was caught by the master with the cover of the pan. This opened the pupil's mind to the secrets of the art, which had hitherto been kept from him. He then for the first time really appreciated the unparalleled kindness of the master.'[1]

The pupil must develop a new sense or, more

[1] Suzuki, Daisetz Teitaro, *Zen Buddhism and its Influence on Japanese Culture*, pp. 7, 8.

accurately, a new alertness of all his senses, which will enable him to avoid dangerous thrusts as though he could feel them coming. Once he has mastered this art of evasion, he no longer needs to watch with undivided attention the movements of his opponent, or even of several opponents at once. Rather, he sees and feels what is going to happen, and at that same moment he has already avoided its effect without there being 'a hair's breadth' between perceiving and avoiding. This, then, is what counts: a lightning reaction which has no further need of conscious observation. In this respect at least the pupil makes himself independent of all conscious purpose. And that is a great gain.

What is very much more difficult and of truly decisive importance is the task of stopping the pupil from thinking and spying out how he can best come at his opponent. Actually, he should clear his mind of the thought that he has to do with an opponent at all and that it is a matter of life and death.

To begin with, the pupil understands these instructions—and he can hardly do otherwise—as meaning that it is sufficient for him to refrain from observing and thinking about the behaviour of his opponent. He takes this non-observation very seriously and controls himself at every step. But he fails to notice that, by concentrating his attention on himself, he inevitably sees himself as the combatant who has at all costs to avoid watching his opponent. Do what he may, he still has him secretly in mind. Only in appearance has he detached himself from him, and the more he endeavours to forget him the more tightly he binds himself to him.

It takes a good deal of very subtle psychological guidance to convince the pupil that fundamentally he has gained nothing by this shift of attention. He must learn to disregard himself as resolutely as he disregards his opponent, and to become, in a radical sense, self-regardless, purposeless. Much patience, much heart-breaking practice is needed, just as in archery. But once this practice has led to the goal the last trace of self-regard vanishes in sheer purposelessness.

This state of purposeless detachment is followed automatically by a mode of behaviour which bears a surprising resemblance to the previous stage of instinctive evasion. Just as, at that stage, there was not a hair's breadth between perceiving the intended thrust and evading it, so now there is no time lag between evasion and action. At the moment of evasion the combatant reaches back to strike, and in a flash the deadly stroke has fallen, sure and irresistible. It is as if the sword wielded itself, and just as we say in archery that 'It' takes aim and hits, so here 'It' takes the place of the ego, availing itself of a facility and a dexterity which the ego only acquires by conscious effort. And here too 'It' is only a name for something which can neither be understood nor laid hold of, and which only reveals itself to those who have experienced it.

Perfection in the art of swordsmanship is reached, according to Takuan, when the heart is troubled by no more thought of I and You, of the opponent and his sword, of one's own sword and how to wield it—no more thought even of life and death. 'All is emptiness: your own self, the flashing sword, and the arms that wield it. Even the thought of emptiness is no longer there.' From this absolute emptiness, states Takuan, 'comes the most wondrous unfoldment of doing'.

What is true of archery and swordsmanship also applies to all the other arts. Thus, mastery in ink-painting is only attained when the hand, exercising perfect control over technique, executes what hovers before the mind's eye at the same moment as the mind begins to form it, without there being a hair's breadth between. Painting then becomes spontaneous calligraphy. Here again the painter's instructions might be: spend ten years observing bamboos, become a bamboo yourself, then forget everything and—paint.

The swordmaster is an unself-conscious as the beginner. The nonchalance which he forfeited at the beginning of his instruction he wins back again at the end as an indestructible characteristic. But, unlike the beginner, he holds himself in reserve, is quiet and unassuming, without the least desire to show off. Between the stages of apprenticeship and mastership there lie long and eventful years of untiring practice. Under the influence of Zen his proficiency becomes spiritual, and he himself, grown ever freer through spiritual struggle, is transformed. The sword, which has now become his 'soul', no longer rests lightly in its scabbard. He draws it only when unavoidable. Thus it may easily happen that he avoids combat with an unworthy opponent, a cockscomb who brags about his muscles, accepting the charge of cowardice with smiling indifference; though on the other hand, out of esteem for an opponent, he will insist on a combat which cannot bring anything but an honourable death to the latter. These are the sentiments that govern the ethos of the Samurai, the incomparable 'path of chivalry' known as Bushido. For, higher than anything else, higher than fame, victory and even life, stands the 'sword of truth' which guides him and judges him.

Like the beginner the swordmaster is fearless, but, unlike him, he grows daily less and less accessible to fear. Years of unceasing meditation have taught him that life and death are at bottom the same and belong to the same stratum of fact. He no longer knows what fear of life and terror of death are. He lives—and this is thoroughly characteristic of Zen—happily enough in the world, but ready at any time to quit it without being in the least disturbed by the thought of death. It is not for nothing that the Samurai have chosen for their truest symbol the fragile cherry blossom. Like a petal dropping in the morning sunlight and floating serenely to earth, so must the fearless detach himself from life, silent and inwardly unmoved.

To be free from the fear of death does not mean pretending to oneself, in one's good hours, that one will not tremble in the face of death, and that there is nothing to fear. Rather, he who masters both life and death is free from fear of any kind to the extent that he is no longer capable of experiencing what fear feels like. Those who do not know the power of rigorous and protracted meditation cannot judge of the self-conquests it makes possible. At any rate the perfected Master betrays his fearlessness at every turn, not in words, but in his whole demeanour: one has only to look at him to be profoundly affected by it. Unshakable fearlessness as such already amounts to mastery, which, in the nature of things, is realized only by the few. As proof of this I shall quote a passage from the *Hagakure*, which dates from about the middle of the seventeenth century:

'Yagyu Tagjima-no-kami was a great swordsman and teacher in the art to the Shogun of the time, Tokugawa Iyemitsu. One of the personal guards of the Shogun one day came to Tajima-no-kami wishing to be trained in fencing. The master said, "As I observe, you seem to be a master of fencing yourself; pray tell me to what school you belong, before we enter into the relationship of teacher and pupil."

'The guardsman said, "I am ashamed to confess that I have never learned the art".

' "Are you going to fool me? I am teacher to the honourable Shogun himself, and I know my judging eye never fails."

' "I am sorry to defy your honour, but I really know nothing."

'This resolute denial on the part of the visitor made the swordsmaster think for a while, and he finally said, "If you say so, it must be so; but still I am sure you are a master of something, though I do not know of what."

' "If you insist, I will tell you. There is one thing of which I can say I am complete master. When I was still a boy, the thought came upon me that as a Samurai I ought in no circumstances to be afraid of death, and I have grappled with the problem of death now for some years, and finally the problem of death ceased to worry me. May this be at what you hint?"

' "Exactly!" exclaimed Tajima-no-kami. "That is what I mean. I am glad that I made no mistake in my judgment. For the ultimate secrets of swordsmanship also lie in being released from the thought of death. I have trained ever so many hundreds of my pupils along this line, but so far none of them really deserve the final certificate for swordsmanship. You need no technical training, you are already a master." [1]

Since ancient times, the practice hall where the swordsman's art is learned has been called the 'Place of Enlightenment'.

. Every Master who practises an art moulded by Zen is like a flash of lightning from the cloud of all-encompassing Truth. This Truth is present in the free movement of his spirit, and he meets it again, in 'It', as his own original and nameless essence. He meets this essence over and over again as his own being's utmost possibilities, so that the Truth assumes for him—and for others through him—a thousand shapes and forms.

In spite of the unexampled discipline to which he has patiently and humbly subjected himself he is still a long way from being so permeated and irradiated by Zen that he is sustained by it in everything he does, so that his life knows only good hours. The supreme freedom has still not become a necessity for him.

If he is irresistibly driven towards this goal, he must set out on his way again, take the road to the artless art. He must dare to leap into the Origin, so

[1] Suzuki, Daisetz Teitaro, *Zen Buddhism and its Influence on Japanese Culture*, pp. 46, 47.

as to live by the Truth and in the Truth, like one who has become one with it. He must become a pupil again, a beginner; conquer the last and steepest stretch of the way, undergo new transformations. If he survives its perils, then is his destiny fulfilled: face to face he beholds the unbroken Truth, the Truth beyond all truths, the formless Origin of origins, the Void which is the All, is absorbed into it and from it emerges reborn.

PENGUIN

ARKANA

NEW AGE BOOKS FOR MIND, BODY & SPIRIT

A SELECTION OF TITLES

Neal's Yard Natural Remedies
Susan Curtis, Romy Fraser and Irene Kohler

Natural remedies for common ailments from the pioneering Neal's Yard Apothecary Shop. An invaluable resource for everyone wishing to take responsibility for their own health, enabling you to make your own choice from homeopathy, aromatherapy and herbalism.

The Healing Power of Mind   Tulku Thondup

Healing meditation, based on the ancient techniques of Buddhist practice, can help everyone to attain a loving, confident attitude and a state of balance and harmony, releasing anxieties and worries and leading to a more relaxed state of being. 'For many years I have dreamed of a book like this' Sogyal Rinpoche

Jesus the Son of Man   Kahlil Gibran

Gibran's inspired portrayal of Christ through the eyes of those who knew him depicts the many aspects of his character: as a carpenter, as a physician, as a wise and tolerant man, as a worker of miracles and as a teacher. Above all, Gibran reveals Jesus's essential humanity. 'The work of a true poet' *Sunday Times*

Power of the Witch   Laurie Cabot

In fascinating detail, Laurie Cabot describes the techniques and rituals involved in charging tools, brewing magical potions and casting vigorous, tantalizing spells. Intriguing and accessible, this taboo-shattering guide will educate and enlighten even the most sceptical reader in the ways of an ancient faith that has much to offer today's world.

PENGUIN

ARKANA

NEW AGE BOOKS FOR MIND, BODY & SPIRIT

A SELECTION OF TITLES

On Love Jacob Needleman

Using a beguiling mixture of mysticism, spirituality and philosophical thought, Jacob Needleman's book takes us from the everyday ups and downs of love, through its role in culture and morality, and on to a notion of love that can reach beyond the mundanities of ordinary existence.

A Separate Reality Carlos Castaneda

In the second book in his astounding journey into the world of sorcery, Castaneda resumes the apprenticeship begun in *The Teachings of Don Juan Carlos* and continues his struggle to become a Man of Knowledge. 'A rare phenomenon, a sequel that proves more exciting than its bestselling predecessor' *Guardian*

A Time to Heal Beata Bishop

The inspiring story of a woman's triumph over life-threatening disease – through an unorthodox therapy. When Beata Bishop's cancer spread into the lymphatic system, she rejected the options of surgery or 'wait-to-die' and travelled to the Gerson clinic in Mexico, for therapy based on optimum nutrition and thorough detoxification. Over a decade later, she is fit and well, enjoying life to the full.

Tao Te Ching Lao Tzu
The Richard Wilhelm Edition

Encompassing philosophical speculation and mystical reflection, the *Tao Te Ching* has been translated more often than any other book except the Bible, and more analysed than any other Chinese classic. Richard Wilhelm's acclaimed 1910 translation is here made available in English.